LIFE BOOKS

Managing Editor
Robert Sullivan

Director of Photography
Barbara Baker Burrows

Creative Director
Anke Stohlmann

Deputy Picture Editor
Christina Lieberman

Writer-Reporter
Michelle DuPré

Copy Editors
Barbara Gogan, Parlan McGaw

Photo Associate
Sarah Cates

Consulting Picture Editors
Mimi Murphy (Rome),
Tala Skari (Paris)

Editorial Director
Stephen Koepp

Editorial Operations Director
Michael Q. Bullerdick

EDITORIAL OPERATIONS

Richard K. Prue (Director), Brian
Fellows (Manager), Richard Shaffer
(Production), Keith Aurelio, Charlotte
Coco, Tracey Eure, Kevin Hart, Mert
Kerimoglu, Rosalie Khan, Patricia
Koh, Marco Lau, Brian Mai, Po Fung
Ng, Rudi Papiri, Robert Pizaro,
Barry Pribula, Clara Renauro, Katy
Saunders, Hia Tan, Vaune Trachtman

TIME HOME ENTERTAINMENT

President Richard Fraiman

**Vice President, Business Development &
Strategy** Steven Sandonato

Executive Director, Marketing Services
Carol Pittard

Executive Director, Retail & Special Sales
Tom Mifsud

Executive Publishing Director Joy Butts

**Director, Bookazine Development &
Marketing** Laura Adam

Finance Director Glenn Buonocore

Associate Publishing Director
Megan Pearlman

Assistant General Counsel Helen Wan

Assistant Director, Special Sales
Ilene Schreider

Book Production Manager Suzanne Janso

Design & Prepress Manager
Anne-Michelle Gallero

Brand Manager Roshni Patel

Associate Prepress Manager
Alex Voznesenskiy

Assistant Brand Manager
Stephanie Braga

Special thanks: Christine Austin,
Katherine Barnet, Jeremy Biloon,
Jim Childs, Susan Chodakiewicz,
Rose Cirrincione, Lauren Hall Clark,
Jacqueline Fitzgerald, Christine Font,
Jenna Goldberg, Hillary Hirsch, David
Kahn, Amy Mangus, Robert Marasco,
Kimberly Marshall, Catherine Mayer,
Amy Migliaccio, Nina Mistry, Dave
Rozzelle, Adriana Tierno, Vanessa Wu

ISBN 13: 1-61893-029-X
ISBN 10: 978-1-61893-029-3
Library of Congress Control Number:
2012937067

Vol. 12, No. 11 • June 15, 2012

"LIFE" is a registered trademark of
Time Inc.

We welcome your comments and
suggestions about LIFE Books. Please
write to us at: LIFE Books,
Attention: Book Editors,
PO Box 11016,
Des Moines, IA 50336-1016

If you would like to order any of our
hardcover Collector's Edition books,
please call us at 1-800-327-6388.
(Monday through Friday, 7:00 a.m.—
8:00 p.m. or Saturday, 7:00 a.m.—
6:00 p.m. Central Time).

Page 1 On June 3, in the marquee
event, the royal barge *Spirit of
Chartwell* plies the Thames.
Robert Todd/Daily Mail/Zuma

Pages 2–3 Schoolchildren, 650 strong,
enjoy a Jubilee street fair in
Gravesend, County of Kent. *Grant
Falvey/London News Pictures/Zuma*

This page The Diamond Jubilee Medal.
Tristan Gregory/Camera Press, London

Jubilee!

Queen Elizabeth II

60 YEARS ON THE THRONE

A Royal Life

t couldn't dampen spirits. Not a bit. That's what everyone was saying about the rain—sometimes a drizzle, sometimes a downpour—that moved across Great Britain as the United Kingdom celebrated with a four-day weekend of pageants and pub crawls, parades and prayers, fetes and festivities, 9,700 street parties from the top of Scotland to the tip of Cornwall (more than twice as many open-air revels as were authorized during last year's wedding of Wills and Kate), a historic flotilla on the River Thames and yet another grand tour of the city by coach, with the hallmark hand-wave semaphoring endlessly. Matt Dobson, a British weatherman, had forewarned, "Keep your brolly handy," but many didn't care. Yes, the prime minister, David Cameron, ordered that his Big Lunch scheduled for outside 10 Downing Street be moved indoors, but the mass of his countrymen—and the queen herself, 86 years young—were made of sterner stuff. "It made me proud to be British,"

ELIZABETH'S LONG JOURNEY: The image above was taken from an archival film entitled Royal Road *that was shot during an auto ride around the grounds of Windsor Castle in 1941. Princess Elizabeth is second from right, and her kid sister, Princess Margaret, is at right; their father, King George VI, and mother, Queen Elizabeth, are also in the car. Opposite: On June 3, 2012, Queen Elizabeth II is transported by launch to the royal barge to take her place in the Thames Diamond Jubilee Pageant, still waving that certain way.*

Sandra Evans, 68, a retired shopworker from East London told Reuters as she stood wrapped—and rapt—in a thoroughly sodden British flag. She was cheek by jowl with 1.2 million other citizens and foreigners, all hoping for a glimpse of the grand flotilla on the Thames. "It'll be a long time before London has another day like this."

Indeed. It had been 115 years since Britannia's last royal Diamond Jubilee, that of Queen Victoria, in 1897. The likelihood that two queens from the same family would each celebrate six decades on the throne, more than a century apart, would be a bet even the most brazen British bookmaker wouldn't post. Another bet that might've looked dodgy as this second Jubilee began: that the focus would remain intently on Elizabeth. Sir Paul McCartney was going to star at the big concert, and surely William or Harry or Kate or—who knows?—Pippa or Fergie's daughters would steal the show.

But no. This was all about one woman, whose story is told in full in the pages that follow. She had come so far, seen so much. Last week, citing the Jubilee and feeling well about itself, Buckingham Palace released some new old images, including a charming one of Elizabeth, waving from a car in 1941. She was in her midteens, and the world was in a bad way. Whether Great Britain would survive the war could not be said, so what could this girl have guessed at the time? Perhaps that she might be queen one day, if there was still an England. But never that the United Kingdom would undergo such upheavals as it did. Never that her own family would suffer through scandals and tragedies. Never the annus horribilis, or the movies and books made about the Windsors. Never the fact that, through perseverance and a firm sense of duty, she would emerge at the end, more beloved than ever, a queen for the ages.

She couldn't have bet on any of that.

Had she chosen to place a safe wager, it might have been on London's weather, which—try as it might—couldn't dampen spirits. Not a bit.

"Long to reign over us

ON JUNE 3, FIREWORKS over Tower
Bridge mark the end of the Thames
Diamond Jubilee Pageant. The drawbridge
had been raised to its full height in salute
as the royal barge passed beneath.

God save the queen"

AT A STREET PARTY to celebrate the Jubilee in London's Fulham neighborhood, James Burgess, his wife, Katherine, and daughter, Charlotte, applaud a toast that has been raised to the queen, while Jonny Messer, four years old but uncarded, reaches for the Champagne.

ON IMPERIAL WHARF at Chelsea Harbour, the queen begins her trek to the Thames for the centerpiece event of the Jubilee, the thousand-boat flotilla. It is later announced that 419 boats reach Tower Bridge this day, surpassing the world record for largest boat parade, set last year in Germany.

ON JUNE 4, as thousands of their countrymen are packing the grounds around Buckingham Palace for the picnic and concert starring Sir Paul McCartney, Sam and Jack Davies celebrate the Diamond Jubilee in quieter fashion on Carne Beach in Cornwall.

England's Earlier Diamond Jubilee

❦

ONCE THERE WAS a queen who sat upon the throne even longer than Elizabeth II has, and on June 20, 1897, London and all of the empire hailed legendary Victoria. She was of mostly Germanic heritage and the last ruler of the House of Hanover in the United Kingdom, but in fact she began the lineage of English monarchs that has led directly to Elizabeth, and that would restyle itself as "the House of Windsor" when World War I made all things Germanic less than savory to the British.

W AND D DOWNEY/HULTON/GETTY

QUEEN ELIZABETH II **17**

Victoria, who ascended to the throne in 1837 to begin a 63-year reign (the longest to date of any British monarch), was the granddaughter of George III and the niece of King William IV, who immediately preceded her as British sovereign. So she was quite a proper inheritrix of the throne. Since her time, succession at the Palace has been direct: Victoria was followed by her eldest son, who was King Edward VII from 1901 to 1910 (the Edwardian Era); Edward was succeeded by his son George, who became George V (1910 to 1936, and the man who oversaw the renaming of the clan as "Windsor"); George was very briefly succeeded by his elder son, Edward VIII, who abdicated after a scandal caused by his love for a twice-divorced American; Edward's departure yielded the throne to his brother, who would become George VI, of *The King's Speech* fame. This George would father two girls: Elizabeth, who still wears the crown after 60 years, and Margaret. Elizabeth and Margaret's mother, also named Elizabeth, would gain renown during World War II for the stoic, inspirational courage she displayed alongside her husband, and would be cherished in her older age as the endearingly cute, hat-wearing Queen Mum. That is the Windsors in a nutshell, and the route that led from the reign of one exceedingly long-lived queen to that of her great-great-granddaughter. Certainly when these pictures were made in June of 1897, it never could have been supposed that 115 years later, the precise same family would be celebrating another of its daughters' Diamond Jubilee.

OPPOSITE PAGE, top, preparations on London's Park Lane for Victoria's Jubilee. At bottom, Westminster Bridge during the festivities. This page, from top: Victoria with the royal family; in the coach on the great day; the procession outside St. Paul's Cathedral for a service of thanksgiving; the British tradition of street parties, this one filling Market Place in Wisbech, Cambridgeshire. Victoria's Jubilee represented a public display by a queen who had withdrawn from public life after the death of her husband, Albert, in 1861. When she acceded to Colonial Secretary Joseph Chamberlain's suggestion that her Jubilee be made into a fantastic festival of the British Empire, the joy was general.

The Girl Who Would Be Queen

DURING PRINCESS ELIZABETH'S *first decade, there was no expectation that she would sit upon the throne one day. She was a sweet, pretty girl being schooled at home to contribute to society, but not to rule. After all, her father stood behind his older brother in line of succession. But then, in less than a year, in 1936, just as Elizabeth was turning 10 years old, everything changed.*

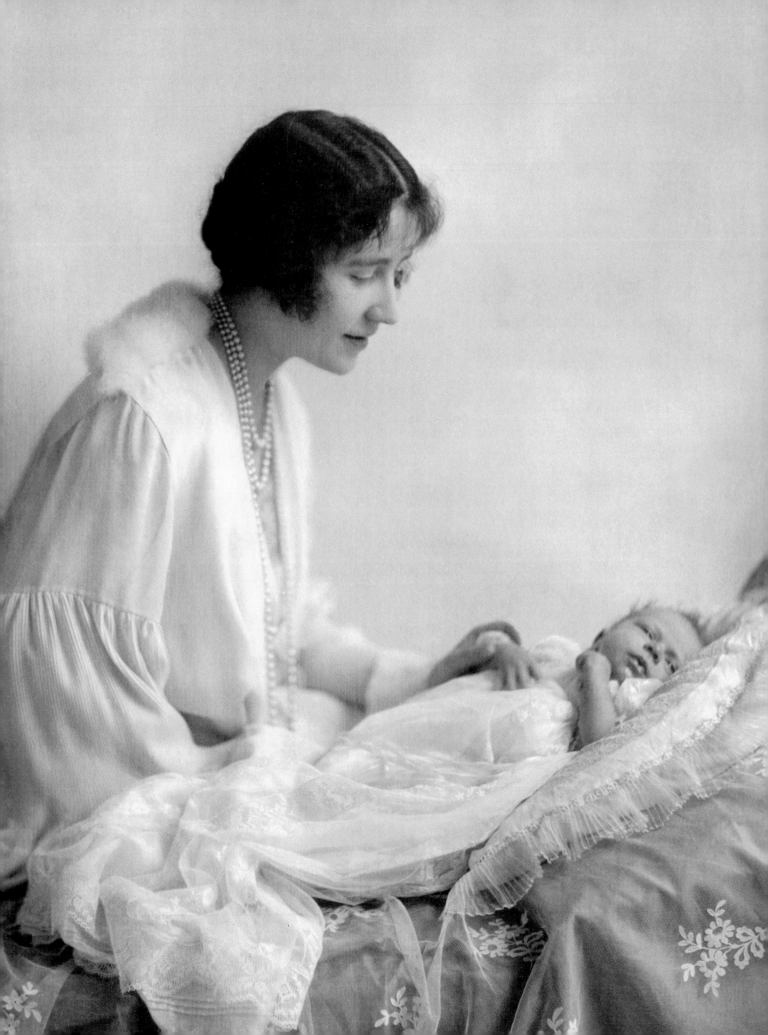

UNDERWOOD & UNDERWOOD/CORBIS

Princess Elizabeth Alexandra Mary of the House of Windsor was born on April 21, 1926, to Prince Albert, Duke of York (the future King George VI) and the former Elizabeth Bowes-Lyon, both of whom are seen in these pictures with the first of their two daughters. The delivery took place at her maternal grandfather's home on Bruton Street in the fashionable Mayfair section of London. She was baptized into the Anglican Church in a private chapel at Buckingham Palace in May, then she was on her way. Her education and that of her sister, Princess Margaret, who joined the family in 1930, was overseen by the girls' mother and their governess Marion "Crawfie" Crawford. By all accounts, Lilibet, as she was called around the house, was a good girl: studious, sensible and with a pronounced attitude of level-headedness. None other than Winston Churchill pronounced Elizabeth, after meeting the little royal when she was but two and a half years old, "a character. She has an air of authority and reflectiveness astonishing in an infant." This is not to say she was an entirely serious or dour child. She was dutiful, yes, but liked to play, and loved animals, particularly dogs and horses. (It seems that not a decade has passed in Elizabeth's long life without the release of photographs featuring her corgis.) Her Royal Highness Princess Elizabeth of York was immediately third in the line of succession to the throne, with her uncle Edward and her own father ahead of her, but during her early girlhood the general assumption was that Edward would wear the crown and probably have his own children somewhere along the way, or that Elizabeth's mother might one day give birth to a son, a male heir who would then leap over her in line. As we now know, things got complicated in 1936 and Elizabeth was quickly set up as monarch-to-be. Edward did succeed his father when George V died that year, but within months his love affair with the divorced American socialite Wallis Simpson blew up into a great scandal and a constitutional crisis. Edward chose Mrs. Simpson over the throne, and upon his abdication Elizabeth's father was made king. The girl Elizabeth was, overnight, heiress presumptive.

IN THE PHOTOGRAPHS opposite and above, the infant Elizabeth is seen with her parents. Below, she is now a toddler, age three. As we know, the British monarchy, since before Victoria's day, exerts no real power; the prime minister is in charge. And yet, most Britons feel they have been lucky to have had George VI and Elizabeth II as a steadying influence following the chaos of the Edward episode—particularly during the dark days of war. That the royals and the scandal-prone House of Windsor survived the 20th century at all is largely the doing of this father-and-daughter combination.

REX USA

MARY EVANS PICTURE LIBRARY

BETTMANN/CORBIS

MARY EVANS PICTURE LIBRARY

AS HAS BEEN MENTIONED and will shortly be emphasized, World War II and its outcome would represent the signature chapter of George VI's tenure, much as it would represent the ultimate triumph of Winston Churchill's long and episodic military and political career. Meantime, however, there was a family for George and Elizabeth to raise, and they were reputedly attentive and caring parents—never something to be assumed when dealing with royals. On the opposite page, at top left, the Duke of York, only months away from becoming king in 1936, and his family (Elizabeth at left, Margaret at right) frolic with their pooches, Scrummy, Mimsy, Dookie, Jane, Stiffy and, held by Mum, Choo-Choo. At top right, the Windsor sisters heave-ho. Below, a relatively early version of what will be an endless stream of images bearing the caption "Elizabeth with Corgi." Above: The family, with the girls up front, on the day of Dad's coronation. He was a reluctant king, a man who dreaded public speaking because of his stammer, but a dutiful Briton who realized the country needed no further distractions after Edward's escapade and with war looming. As the family moved from the private life at their London home on Piccadilly to Buckingham Palace, Albert took the name King George VI to show continuity with his father, skipping any association with Edward whatsoever.

DURING THE BLITZ and for much of World War II, the Windsor parents tried to make a show of staying at Buckingham Palace whenever they could to bolster the spirits of their subjects in London. The girls, Elizabeth and Margaret, were largely relocated to Windsor Castle outside the city, and spent a lot of time on the family's other, even more remote estates. But pictures of them, too, were circulated in an effort to show that life goes on, and that there will always be an England. Above: Elizabeth feeds an elephant at the London Zoo circa 1940. Opposite: With a horse during harvest time at the royal Sandringham Estate in Norfolk in 1943. Interestingly, Diana Spencer, later Lady Di, would be born in a house on the Sandringham property in 1961.

THE NAZIS having swept through much of Europe—taking even France—brought the war to London with a brutal series of bombing missions that became known as the Blitz. Winston Churchill worked hard to inspire his countrymen's will to resist, and just as hard to get like-thinking nations, particularly the United States, to support the British cause and even enter the fray. The Windsors did what they could whenever they could, and George VI developed a surprising and respectful relationship with Churchill, who kept him apprised of matters. The Girl Guides, a sister organization to the Boy Scouts, made sure to form the 1st Buckingham Palace Company so that Elizabeth and Margaret might interact with girls of their own age, and Elizabeth, predictably, eventually became patrol leader; at left, third from top, she writes a message to be sent by courier pigeon to Lady Baden-Powell, widow of the Scouting movement founder, during "Thinking Day" activities in February 1943 as Princess Margaret attends. The year before, on her 16th birthday, she made her first solo appearance representing the Crown when visiting the Grenadier Guards, but even earlier she and Margaret (second from top) had been engaged in efforts to buck up the citizenry. The two appeared on the BBC's Children's Hour *radio program in 1940, and Elizabeth told other kids who had been evacuated during the Blitz, "We are trying to do all we can to help our gallant sailors, soldiers and airmen, and we are trying, too, to bear our own share of the danger and sadness of war. We know, every one of us, that in the end all will be well." Late in the war, she was trained as a driver and mechanic (left, bottom) and was promoted to honorary Junior Commander but did not see action. Her parents, meantime, did even more. Her father (left, top) confronted his stammer and spoke directly to his people when not otherwise setting an example. Opposite, top: The Blitz began on September 7, 1940; more than 400 Londoners were killed, and four days after the first bombs dropped, Queen Elizabeth, with King George just behind her, inspects air raid damage at Buckingham Palace. Two days after this, German bombs destroyed the palace's chapel while the king and queen were in residence; they narrowly avoided death. Lord Hailsham suggested that even Windsor Castle wasn't safe enough for Elizabeth and Margaret and that the princesses should be sent to Canada. The queen replied, "The children won't go without me. I won't leave the king. And the king will never leave." He never did, and in 1945 he, his family and Churchill celebrated Victory in Europe Day from the balcony of Buckingham Palace (opposite, bottom). Elizabeth and Margaret implored their mother and father to be allowed to mingle with the people filling the streets. "We asked my parents if we could go out and see for ourselves," Queen Elizabeth II recalled years later. "I remember we were terrified of being recognized . . . I remember lines of unknown people linking arms and walking down Whitehall, all of us just swept along on a tide of happiness and relief."*

IAN SMITH

WITH THE WAR OVER, *British smiles were broad again, and it was time for some frivolity. Well, maybe those of the Gorsedd of the Bards of the Isle of Britain would not count their induction ceremonies as frivolous. What in the world is the Gorsedd of the Bards? It is an association that has recognized, since its founding in 1792, generations of worthy Ovates, Bards and Druids (ranks, you see) who have made distinguished contributions to Welsh literature, poetry, music and scholarship generally. At the National Eisteddfod, a Welsh language and culture festival, new initiates are brought forth—as Elizabeth is, above, in 1946. The following year, she is caught playing tag with midshipmen as they cross the Atlantic during one of her formal forays on behalf of the Crown.*

Philip
1927

Philip 1930

MEANTIME, a handsome young gentleman, also of a royal family, was growing up—first in Greece, then elsewhere on the Continent and eventually in England. He was born Prince Philip of Greece and Denmark on June 10, 1921, and is seen here, counterclockwise from left, in a sailor suit in 1927, in traditional Greek dress in 1930, and wearing a rakish mien circa 1936. By then, Elizabeth had met Philip, who had British ties and was in fact one of her third cousins through Queen Victoria; before the decade was out, she would be deeply in love. This is Philip's brief biography: As an infant he was seen, but only for one year, as a crucial player in Europe's often dense and confusing royal aristocracy, a network of rulers extending centuries back but under assault in the 19th and 20th centuries. He was a member of the Danish-German House of Schleswig-Holstein-Sonderburg-Glücksburg, and there was certainly a possibility that Prince Philip might be king of Greece one day; his uncle at the time of his birth was King Constantine I. But when Philip was barely a year old, his uncle was forced to abdicate when the war between the Greeks and the Turks went the Turkish way. As the commander of the Greek army and others were executed, Philip's father, Prince Andrew, gathered up his family and fled into exile aboard the British navy's HMS Calypso, *with Philip in a crib made from an orange crate. Places in Germany, Paris and Scotland were stopping points during Philip's boyhood, and then of course England. He joined the Royal Navy at the age of 18 in 1939. By then, he had met the child Elizabeth a couple of times, but in that year, her parents, touring the Royal Naval College at Dartmouth, asked Philip, who was a cadet there, to escort their daughters, Elizabeth and Margaret. Elizabeth, only 13, swooned—and this proved to be more than a schoolgirl's crush. She and Philip began exchanging letters and continued to do so during the war as Philip rose in the ranks after graduating at the top of his Dartmouth corps. By war's end, having seen action in the Allied invasion of Sicily, the Pacific Theater and elsewhere, he had received the Greek War Cross of Valour and been promoted to first lieutenant; he was made commander in 1952; he gave up his dream of a lifelong naval career only after assuming his role as the queen's consort. (Elizabeth II made her husband a Lord High Admiral of the Navy in 2011, and that certainly must have been gratifying to Philip.) After the war, Philip asked Elizabeth to marry him during a stroll at Balmoral. "It was wonderful, magical," Elizabeth later remembered. "I just threw my arms round his neck and kissed him as he held me to him, my feet off the ground." It wasn't until the following spring that George VI grudgingly gave his blessing.*

Elizabeth & Philip

IN EACH OTHER'S EYES, the lovely young princess and the dashing naval officer, seen here in 1946, were absolutely made for each other. In the eyes of many of Elizabeth's countrymen, and in those of her parents, the future queen was made for better prospects. Ah, but true love will find a way.

*Y*ou might think the British public would have cut Philip some slack—valorous in war; quick to renounce his Greek royal titles and become a naturalized Englishman; equally fast in converting from Greek Orthodoxy to Anglicanism. But, no. There were, certainly, complications, and some of them had to do with the recently ended war itself. Between 1929 and 1931, Philip's four sisters had married four German nobles and had moved to their husbands' homeland. In subsequent years, these men were linked to the Nazi party. None other than Elizabeth's own mother, who would later develop an image as the sweet old Queen Mum but who was in fact as tough as nails, privately referred to Philip as "the Hun." "Crawfie" Crawford later expressed the national—and royal—mood succinctly. The Scotswoman published, in 1950, an insider's memoir entitled *The Little Princesses: The Story of the Queen's Childhood by Her Nanny, Marion Crawford.* (This indiscreet book would cost her the friendship of the royal family; Elizabeth II would never speak to her again.) At one point Crawfie wrote: "Some of the King's advisers did not think [Philip] good enough for her. He was a prince without home or kingdom. Some of the papers played long and loud tunes on the string of Philip's foreign origin." There were other things that might have elicited sympathy, but just as easily, in some quarters, led to disquiet. Philip's mother was in an asylum, having been diagnosed with schizophrenia, and his father was living out of an apartment in, of all places, Monte Carlo. In the face of this, the young lovers persevered, and eventually most if not all Britons came around to their side. This was not, in the end, anything like the Edward VIII–Wallis Simpson *affaire d'amour.* This was a union of two young people who had distinguished themselves during the recent global crisis. Winston Churchill declared the ultimately inevitable wedding a "bright ray of color on the hard gray road we have to travel."

HERE ARE Princess Elizabeth and Lieutenant Mountbatten (Philip's new British surname) dancing together publicly for the first time. They are attending a ball at the Assembly Rooms in Edinburgh, Scotland, on July 16, 1947. Mutual admiration is evident. As the English and others say, the proof is in the pudding. If the world needs to know that the two were right in '47 and their detractors were wrong, please consider: Their marriage will have lasted 65 mostly happy years come November 2012, and they can still be caught looking at one another in precisely this fashion.

MARY EVANS PICTURE LIBRARY

FRANK SCHERSCHEL

MARY EVANS PICTURE LIBRARY

PIX INC.

BETTMAN/CORBIS

THE WEDDING takes place in Westminster Abbey on November 20, 1947, Elizabeth radiant in a white satin dress with garlands of pearl orange blossom, syringa, jasmine and White Rose of York. Postwar Great Britain is not yet firmly back on its feet, as Winston Churchill's comment on the previous pages indicates, and Elizabeth requires ration coupons to pay for the material in the gown, which is designed by Norman Hartnell. Still, there is pomp, circumstance and not a little opulence. More than 2,500 wedding gifts from around the world fill Buckingham Palace, to which 150 select guests repair after the ceremony for continuing festivities. (Just above, the many thousands that throng the palace for a glimpse of the newlyweds.) Not among the 150 special invitees are Philip's three surviving sisters or England's former King Edward VIII—Elizabeth's uncle—who had indeed married the former Mrs. Simpson, thereby confirming in the eyes of many British his thoroughgoing disgrace.

BARON/CAMERA PRESS, LONDON

AP

BUILDING A ROYAL FAMILY: *Philip and Elizabeth's four children include Prince Charles (born in 1948, at top; in his father's arms at right; and checking out a fish pond at Balmoral, above, with his aunt Margaret and his grandmother and mother) and Princess Anne (born in 1950, in her mother's arms at right). A decade will pass before Prince Andrew is born, and Prince Edward's subsequent arrival will complete the family. Today, Charles is heir apparent to the throne and his and Diana's sons, William and Harry, are second and third.*

PA

She Takes the Throne

IT IS 1952: Unbeknownst to his nation, George VI is suffering from lung cancer. However, it is a coronary thrombosis that claims him on February 6. The 25-year-old Princess Elizabeth, who, with Philip, is vacationing in Kenya at the start of an international tour, immediately becomes Queen Elizabeth II. She hastens to London to grieve with family, to help with funeral arrangements and to prepare for her formal coronation. The royal orb and sceptre are being polished to a brilliant sheen.

As the 1940s turned to the '50s, Elizabeth was being brought increasingly to the fore. She went to bat for her father at various ceremonies, and in the fall of '51 toured Canada and the U.S. representing the Crown. She carried with her a draft accession declaration. If the man in the street didn't know how ill George VI was, the Palace certainly did. And then the king died, after 16 enormously popular years on the throne. Philip told his wife the news in Kenya, and immediately thereafter her private secretary asked her what her regnal name would be. She said that "of course" she would remain Elizabeth. Upon her return to London, she, Philip and their children, Charles and Anne, moved into Buckingham Palace. The outpouring of emotion over George's death was great and immediate, which Prime Minister Churchill deemed proper: "We cannot at this moment do more than record the spontaneous expression of grief." Theaters across the land closed; the BBC cancelled all but news programming; flags went to half-staff; the U.S. Congress voted to adjourn in honor of the king. The funeral was on February 15, 1952, and then, very quietly and decorously, attention turned to what would be another public service, the coronation of Elizabeth. There would be no hurry. She was already, technically, queen. So Elizabeth and the Palace allowed the focus to stay on George and his tenure—"He shared to the end of his reign all the hardships and austerities which evil days imposed on the brave British people," said U.S. President Harry S Truman. "In return, he received from the people of the whole Commonwealth a love and devotion which went beyond the usual relationship of a king and his subjects"—and then allowed the sadness to ebb. Eventually, even as the seamstresses were already at work, a date was chosen for Elizabeth to be crowned: June 2, 1953.

BETTMANN/CORBIS

HULTON-DEUTSCH/CORBIS

ON THESE PAGES, the prep, the pomp and the pooped. The lengthy wait for a coronation was planned to properly respect the memory of King George, and also in order to make careful and elaborate preparations for a truly grand celebration. Westminster Abbey was thoroughly decked out, and so would be the queen: Elizabeth's coronation gown bore an emblem from each Commonwealth realm, from a New Zealand fern to an Irish shamrock. The world had entered the modern age and the whole affair, minus the anointing itself and the communion, was televised globally. Twenty million Brits watched, along with millions more throughout the Commonwealth. Above: Prince Charles has a front row seat for all the commotion, but he is plum tuckered out as he weathers the long ceremony along with his grandmother and aunt.

CORNELL CAPA

JOHN CHILLINGWORTH/PICTURE POST/GETTY

ANOTHER REASON for the hiatus between accession and coronation was the hope that a day in late spring might deliver good weather—a hope rekindled in the Diamond Jubilee year of 2012, when June 2 again became the target. In the event, back when, the weather in London was typically gray, though this did little to dampen the enthusiasm of the 3 million subjects who filled the city's streets, making prime viewing spots prized (above). If a person wasn't at a block party (right, on Swinbrook Road, Kensington) or watching on the telly, he or she was hoping to catch the barest glimpse of the queen in the Gold State Coach, traveling in a long and glorious military cortege through the city. The brilliant parade, featuring the different colors and styles of 29,200 uniforms—Rhodesian soldiers in short pants, Hindus in turbans—passed through Whitehall, Trafalgar Square, Pall Mall, St. James's Street and Piccadilly (Elizabeth's old neighborhood), into Hyde Park, under Marble Arch, down Oxford Street and into Regent Street, again through Trafalgar Square, and finally under the Admiralty Arch and up the Mall to Buckingham Palace, where 8,000 guests would take part in the revels.

MARY EVANS PICTURE LIBRARY

Portfolio: *Lisa Sheridan*

The privileges of royalty are many. Among the slightest, perhaps, is to have one's picture taken as one wishes, and by whom one chooses. The Windsors employed favorite painters and photographers; at LIFE, we are dedicated to the camera, so we choose to pause here in the telling of Elizabeth's life to focus on three artists of the lens—Lisa Sheridan, Cecil Beaton and Yousuf Karsh—who were admired by Elizabeth, and who beautifully recorded her story through the years. These were the polar opposites of the paparazzi we associate with royal photography today. They were invited in, most graciously, and they rendered the behind-the-scenes of Palace life and the intimate, surprising moments—as well as the formal, stunningly lovely portraits. Enjoy.

ON THE OPPOSITE PAGE is Elizabeth in 1940. In her autobiography, From Cabbages to Kings, *Lisa Sheridan talks about how, after a somewhat bohemian upbringing in England, then Russia, then back in England, she married Jimmy Sheridan, who would become her partner in photography, and how, one day, her mother brought her on a visit to the home of the Duke and Duchess of York at 145 Piccadilly, where Sheridan's mother's friend was a servant. During the visit, Lisa first saw the infant Princess Elizabeth.*

IN HER MEMOIRS, Sheridan remembers shooting— photographically—the royal corgis for a book on dogs, then after the pictures appear unlawfully in the national press, falling into a complaining correspondence with the Duke and Duchess of York— Elizabeth's parents. This leads, says Sheridan, to picture sessions at the Royal Lodge in Windsor Great Park. From 1936 forward, the duke, who would soon enough become King George VI, and his young family enjoy Sheridan's company and her photography. The regular sittings, such as the one including a shot of Elizabeth at the piano (opposite), will anchor best-selling books. At top, above, are the princesses Elizabeth and Margaret in 1936, playing outside the Royal Lodge in Windsor in an oversized playhouse, a gift from the people of Wales. Sheridan mostly focused on the girls and their corgis—it's what the public wanted—but in 1946 she made an altogether charming photograph of the king and his elder daughter, who will be queen (right).

Portfolio: Cecil Beaton

f Lisa Sheridan was a somewhat accidental photographer from a family on society's fringe, Cecil Beaton—later, Sir Cecil Beaton—was to the aristocracy and to the aristocratic aesthetic born. He was raised in the London borough of Hampstead by his well-to-do parents; his father had made a fortune in the timber business. His dad was also an amateur actor and had met Beaton's mother when she was appearing in a play—so, though upper class, they were a bit bohemian as well. Beaton would become not only one of the 20th century's most celebrated fashion and portrait photographers but a sought-after painter and interior designer and a preeminent costume designer for theatrical productions and the movies. He was named to the International Best-Dressed Hall of Fame (the peacock was not acknowledged) and won three Academy Awards. Meantime, he became a favorite of the Windsors.

BEATON HARDLY began with Princess Elizabeth—earlier, he had charmed and made charming portraits of her mother, who is remembered as Beaton's favorite royal subject (he once secured her handkerchief as a keepsake after a successful session)—but he realized early on how he might accentuate Elizabeth's beauty. Opposite is one of his renderings, in a treatment just shy of Maxfield Parrish. On the following pages: more intimate, then even more formal.

CAMERA PRESS, LONDON (5)

THESE PHOTOGRAPHS *are self-explanatory, and are meant to show the breadth of Beaton. Elizabeth chose him to make the official coronation portrait, opposite, but earlier had smiled for him with her family, or when encouraging her fellow British citizens as the colonel-in-chief of the Grenadier Guards during World War II. Interestingly, though not apropos (visually) to our book: During that war, Beaton worked in the British Ministry of Information and at one point, during the Blitz, made a famous and touching photograph of three-year-old Eileen Dunne recovering in a hospital. When the picture was published in the United States, which was not yet in the war, the upswell in interventionism was pronounced. Such as Beaton, as well as Churchill, influenced events.*

Portfolio: *Yousuf Karsh*

He was born in the southeastern Ottoman Empire (now Turkey) in 1908, and had a truly hard-bitten youth, during which he lost a sister to famine and survived the global influenza pandemic of 1918. Karsh and his family fled to Syria in 1922, and two years later he was sent to Sherbrooke in Quebec, Canada, where he came under the care of his uncle George Nakash, a photographer. Nakash nurtured Yousuf's career as a portraitist. Karsh became a close friend of the Canadian prime minister, and he came in contact with important Britons. His most famous portrait, from 1941, is of a glowering Winston Churchill—an image that inspired millions to defy the Axis. He also made lovely pictures of the royal family.

ON THE OPPOSITE PAGE, Elizabeth in 1951. As will become clear on the two following pages, Karsh—as opposed to especially Sheridan and even Beaton—was less interested in the causal moments, but in the formal settings. His goal, usually accomplished, was to make beautiful, timeless portraits.

THE PICTURES on these two pages need no captions beyond time frame. Above, in the top row, is Elizabeth in 1951. In the bottom row, Elizabeth and Philip in as close to a "glam shot" as they will ever pose for, and then in 1966. Opposite: The queen, in a moment of reflection, in 1985. All of the pictures on these and the previous 10 pages were seen by (and often approved by) the royal family. But they are hardly unrevealing; they tell us something, even as they are fun to look at. And now, our portfolios done, we return to the "unofficial" photographic record, which is of course substantial because the camera was always trained on the queen of England—as it is today.

The Life of a Queen

NOT ALL—IN FACT, not many—of the duties of a queen are to be desired. Much of her day-to-day is same old, same old. But to place a crown upon the crown of one's own son is an act to be remembered. On July 1, 1969, Elizabeth II, presiding at Caernarfon Castle in Gwynedd, Wales, invests Charles as the Prince of Wales. For fashionistas, and we realize you are many, the queen is obviously Late '60s Adult, while the prince is Eternal Royal/Military Formal: the blue uniform of the Royal Regiment of Wales beneath the purple silk and velvet handwoven mantle and regalia, along with the coronet, sword and ring that had been used in the investiture of the previous Prince of Wales in 1911. Splendid.

A CHANGING WORLD: At top, in 1965, Queen Elizabeth greets American royalty during the dedication ceremony of a British memorial to the late U.S. President John F. Kennedy. She shakes John F. Kennedy Jr.'s hand as Jacqueline Kennedy, Caroline Kennedy, Bobby Kennedy, Ted Kennedy and Jean Smith, sister of the Kennedy lads and eventual U.S. ambassador to Ireland, look on. Above: In 1969, the British royals welcome President Richard Nixon to Buckingham Palace (from left, Anne, Charles, Philip, Nixon and the queen). Opposite, in 1961: Elizabeth and Philip gaze into the pool in front of the Taj Mahal, perhaps wondering how their empire had lost all of these marvelous possessions.

H er nation was delighted—thrilled—to have her. She was both a queen who hearkened to Victoria and a queen for the new world order, and she was smart, pretty and no-nonsense: just what postwar Great Britain needed. Her reign would prove transformative and, at turns, surprisingly tumultuous, none of which had anything much to do with her. Her father had ruled ("ruled" so to speak; the British Empire had long since become a constitutional monarchy) over a community of countries that constituted a true world power, perhaps *the* world power: Many of these realms really were controlled by London (Westminster, if not Buckingham Palace). But when the dust settled after World War II, the United States and the Soviet Union were clearly the new superpowers, and meantime several of Britain's subject nations were maneuvering for independence. (George VI was, for instance, the last emperor of India.) The short of it: The monarchy that Elizabeth's parents had helped save from a fate akin to death became ever more transparently a charade. On top of this, there were the personal travails that sucked up an immense amount of Fleet Street ink: a wandering son, an unwanted daughter-in-law, a woman named Fergie (yet another unwanted daughter-in-law), clandestine tape recordings, a tragic death, a burned-out castle, an Academy Award–winning movie in which Helen Mirren got Elizabeth precisely right and James Cromwell rendered Prince Philip only too well . . . It was all very un-Elizabeth, and it must be said: She handled all of it—all the weight of it, all the detritus—as well as might be humanly possible.

BETTMANN/CORBIS

MIRRORPIX/EVERETT

MARY EVANS PICTURE LIBRARY

SHE HAS ALWAYS loved horses, and, as a daughter of World War II, she has always loved freedom. It can even be said that, although she is a royal, she has had a soft spot for democracy her entire life. Speculations aside, the queen is seen on the opposite page riding on the course at Ascot in 1961, and at right, riding with her friend U.S. President Ronald Reagan on royal horses at Windsor Castle in 1982. Above: The queen offers a bon mot and the President guffaws. Reagan's relations with England could not have been tighter, and his alliance in this period with Prime Minister Margaret Thatcher proved instrumental in the fall of Soviet communism.

DIANA SPENCER: This young woman, so perfect as a princess and perhaps so perfect a future queen in many ways, was so anti-Windsor in other ways that her marriage to Prince Charles in 1981 was doubted from the first by some of Charles's relations, and then denigrated by them in private as Charles and Di sought to find their way. The Prince of Wales and his bride discovered quickly enough that they could not find that way—or any way. They ultimately were unfaithful to each other, and then divorced. Before they did so, Diana would give birth to two fine boys, who today are second and third in line of succession to the British throne, behind Charles. The public's adoration of Lady Di, who instinctively possessed a common touch that seemed as foreign to the Windsors as Antarctica, rendered Queen Elizabeth and Prince Philip gobsmacked. Why in the bloody world do our subjects love her so? No one could give them any kind of answer that might satisfy. The two photos on this page say much: Elizabeth and Diana are doing their best, and are apparently genuinely happy, on the day of the Wedding of the Century, July 29, 1981. Only weeks later, when the royal family visits the village of Braemar in Scotland (above), Diana is already miserable. She hated all things outdoorsy and was particularly unfond of the royal family's estate at Balmoral. The queen loves all things outdoorsy and she loves Balmoral. Balmoral was the final stop of Charles and Di's honeymoon: nice planning. The Windsors' great episode of doom was in progress.

FOR A TIME—unfortunately a very brief time—Charles and Diana's marriage looked to the public like some kind of idyll, and their growing family looked like the ideal nuclear unit (albeit a Royal Nuclear Unit). Still today, as Wills and Harry play their parts in their grandmother's Diamond Jubilee, the boys are glittering and successful world personalities—A-list ambassadors—as well as intrepid members of their nation's military. That they have emerged so strong from the tumult of their parents' union is a credit to them both. That their grandmother survived the Sturm und Drang that attended "Charles-and-Di," and all else during her self-proclaimed "annus horribilis," is a testament to Elizabeth's remarkable fortitude and stoicism. Here we have sunshine before the storm: The Windsors welcome William to the fold. He was born in 1982 and Harry would arrive two years later. Wills would be the good boy and stellar student, graduating from St. Andrews; Harry would be the lovable rascal. Both would be raised principally by their hands-on mother, as Diana would choose their names, their schools, their clothing. The Waleses' home was Kensington Palace, off Hyde Park, and they were happy there. But infidelity would intrude (it was in place at the very outset of the marriage, if Diana's account is to be credited), and the ability to remain husband and wife, even by the letter of the law, became untenable. Diana and the boys continued on at Kensington as Charles's relationship with Camilla Parker Bowles was parsed (with a distinct lack of gentility) by Fleet Street. In 1992, Elizabeth and Philip counseled their eldest son and his princess to reconcile, but although Charles and Diana had proper filial respect, this was a nonstarter. If Elizabeth thought that general affairs at the Palace were bad, she had no idea how much worse they were about to become.

THE WINDSORS had been through much—they had been through Edward VIII!—but they hadn't been through anything like the 1990s. Elizabeth's annus horribilis—her horrible year—was 1992, when her second son, Andrew, separated from his wife, Sarah, better known as Fergie, in March; when her daughter, Anne, divorced her husband, Captain Mark Phillips, in April; when demonstrators in Germany threw eggs at her; when the fact that she didn't pay income taxes became a tabloid issue (an issue rectified when she volunteered to pay); when Charles and Di became an even bigger tabloid issue; when, in November, Windsor Castle burned (above, top and left). On November 24, Elizabeth, at a luncheon at Guildhall given by the Lord Mayor of London ostensibly to celebrate the 40th anniversary of her accession to the throne, and with Prime Minister John Major listening to her sadness (above, top right, at far left), delivers her famous speech delineating the annus horribilis and, uncharacteristically, pleading for understanding. Five years later, well after the marriage of the Waleses has failed, Diana is killed in a car crash in Paris. Elizabeth and Philip are stunned by the great public expressions of sorrow, and the queen is criticized for being slow to react to her people's grief. Above, right: On September 4, she finally acknowledges the flowers at Balmoral, where she and much of her family had been on holiday. Later, pressured, she will return to London and do the same outside Buckingham Palace, where a sea of floral tributes has swelled by the hour. That she and Philip seem to mourn the death of "the People's Princess" only grudgingly will be one of the most commented-upon aspects of Elizabeth's long reign.

DYLAN MARTINEZ/REUTERS

IAN JONES/GAMMA

REUTERS

AFTER SHE WAS past the awful 1990s, after she was past all of that, after her children's lives were reordered—Elizabeth fell back on family, and things were better. Her grandsons by Charles and Diana proved a source of considerable pride. At top, on December 15, 2006, Prince William (wearing the red sash) grins at his grandmother during the Sovereign's Parade at the Royal Military Academy Sandhurst; he is graduating as an army officer and launching his military career. Left: Prince Harry is even less able to hold back as the queen reviews the cadets on April 12, 2006. On the opposite page, top, Charles and Elizabeth are trailed by Charles's second wife, Camilla, Philip, Wills and Harry at a private reception on November 13, 2008, celebrating (a day in advance) Charles's 60th birthday. The hands, bottom, are Elizabeth's and Philip's at the State Opening of Parliament on May 17, 2005.

KIERAN DOHERTY/REUTERS/CORBIS

OF ALL THE RECENT lovely ceremonies, including those attending the Jubilee, none was lovelier than the marriage of Prince William and Kate Middleton on April 29, 2011. The early betting line was that Elizabeth's hat would be yellow, and that safe wager paid out. She wasn't the star this day, but was a solid supporting player. The queen is acknowledged by her grandson and his bride, at top, and, below that, by her eldest son and his wife at Westminster Abbey, where she and Philip had wed nearly 64 years earlier. At right, she and her husband smile at the crowd while the new tradition— the kiss for the crowd at Buckingham Palace—is made manifest. Wills and Kate actually thrilled the crowd with not one but two kisses. Whether Elizabeth and Philip were shocked went unreported, but such wanton behavior was certainly unheard of in their day.

Jubilee!

THE JUBILEE YEAR kicked off in earnest in February, giving the signal that, in 2012, the party in the United Kingdom would go on and on. There would be months of lead-up not only to Queen Elizabeth's big June weekend but to the Olympics, which land in town in late July. Here, on February 6, the King's Troop Royal Horse Artillery offers a 41-gun salute in London's Hyde Park to mark the 60th anniversary of Elizabeth's accession to the throne: one of the first formal declarations that the curtain had been raised on the Jubilee.

UPPA/ZUMA

ROTA/REDUX

DARREN STAPLES/REUTERS

"In this special year, as I dedicate myself anew to your service, I hope we will all be reminded of the power of togetherness and the convening strength of family, friendship and good neighborliness, examples of which I have been fortunate to see throughout my reign and which my family and I look forward to seeing in many forms as we travel throughout the United Kingdom and the wider Commonwealth."

So declares Elizabeth in early 2012, making clear that the game is afoot: Don't wait till June, start partying now. June 2 has been chosen as the date for the Jubilee kickoff, but there is at least a bit of the arbitrary about this. Sixty years ago, remember, King George VI died on February 6, 1952; the cannon salute on the pages previous is a far more accurate marker of Elizabeth becoming queen. Back when, June 2, *1953*, was chosen as a good date for a coronation, not least because it was hoped there might be some nice weather—so this year's festivities, in fact, coincided with the *59th* anniversary of her coronation.

There are commemorative tree plantings, dinners and ceremonies and fetes, and a trip to the Caribbean by Prince Harry that comes off smashingly. Elizabeth today is queen regnant of 16 sovereign states— "Commonwealth realms"—12 of which were colonies or Dominions when she took the throne; travels and acknowledgments in the Jubilee year are therefore widespread. Having been buffeted by various issues over time, she is now the very face of hard-won experience, and says only that the use of public funds for Jubilee events should be minimized throughout the U.K., and no one should be "forced to celebrate."

But, especially on the weekend beginning June 2, millions choose to. And what a party it is!

OPPOSITE: On February 3 at the royal estate in Sandringham, the queen plants a tree as part of the Woodland Trust's Jubilee Woods project, which will see six million more plantings throughout the U.K. This page, from top: Elizabeth receives a bouquet as she arrives in Leicester during her Diamond Jubilee tour; she cuts into a special cake designed by students in Somerset during a Jubilee Country Fayre; and back at Leicester Cathedral, she smiles broadly as flag-waving subjects line the streets and, this day, local politicians offer gushing praise.

ROBIN NUNN/NUNN SYNDICATION/POLARIS

IN PAST YEARS, *Elizabeth spent the specific anniversary of her accession largely in seclusion because of course it also marks the anniversary of her father's death. Not so, this year. She is still at Sandringham, having planted that tree, and this day she travels to nearby King's Lynn, Norfolk, where perhaps 150 fans gather to wave flags and welcome her. The borough's mayor, Colin Sampson, pays tribute to the queen's "dedicated and exemplary service to the people of this country and the Commonwealth," and then presents Elizabeth with a certificate of her father's birth, which took place on the Sandringham Estate in 1895. Later, seen here, Elizabeth visits the 120 students of the Dersingham Infant and Nursery School. They had written to their neighbor in Sandringham the year before, begging a visit, and had heard only two weeks beforehand that she would show. Could that be why they didn't have time to learn "God Save the Queen"? They serenade their monarch instead with "The Time Warp" from* The Rocky Horror Picture Show. *Anything pleases Elizabeth during Jubilee season, and she applauds. Elsewhere, the traditional 41-gun salute is taking place at Hyde Park, 62 guns are fired from the Tower of London and a 21-gun salute is carried out by the 105th Regiment Royal Artillery at Edinburgh Castle in Scotland. Whether any of these packs the wallop of "The Time Warp" by the children of Dersingham Infant and Nursery is debatable.*

STEFAN WERMUTH/REUTERS

OLIVIA HARRIS/REUTERS

OLIVIA HARRIS/REUTERS

EVEN AS THE *festivities progress—multifaith reception at the Archbishop of Canterbury's residence, check; Jubilee address to both houses of Parliament, check; Diamond Jubilee Pageant at Windsor Castle with all those Italian horses (550 horses in all) and Mexican mariachi dancers and New Zealand Maori performers (1,100 performers in all), plus Susan Boyle serenading, check—even as all of this unspools, thousands are working behind the scenes to prepare for June 2. Opposite, another Jubilee event, as the queen is escorted by her granddaughter-in-law, Kate Middleton, at Leicester Cathedral. This page, clockwise from above, the busy bees: At the City & Guilds of London Art School, a student details a decoration for the royal barge that will carry the queen on the River Thames during the June 3 flotilla; a baker works on a marzipan mosaic, a template for a 94-square-foot cake made of 3,120 small cakes, which will be displayed at the Diamond Jubilee Festival in Battersea Park, London, also on June 3; at Wellington Barracks, military tailor Wendy Board alters uniforms to be worn during the fetes; the 94-foot gilded wooden row-barge that will lead the thousand-vessel river pageant—eventually to be named Gloriana—is handcrafted at a top secret location in West London; at the Tower of London, Bruno Peek, pageant master of the Queen's Diamond Jubilee Beacons, poses with the Crystal Diamond that Elizabeth will use on June 4 to light the National Beacon.*

ALEX LENTATI/EVENING STANDARD/ZUMA

STEFAN WERMUTH/REUTERS

AS JUNE 2 *draws closer, it seems members of the royal family are everywhere. The younger generation goes over like gangbusters, Prince Harry wowing the international press with that Jubilee tour of poor precincts in the Caribbean; Kate Middleton spurring sales of coral-colored jeans when she whacks the field hockey ball around with the British Olympic team. (That appearance has to do with the upcoming Games, but Kate is hanging with the queen at the time, so it has overtones of Jubilee.) Even the oldsters do well in this festive season. Polls show Camilla rising in popularity among her countryfolk, a phenomenon not to be considered until recently. Her husband, Prince Charles, perhaps emboldened by all of this bonhomie, executes one of his goofy turns and reads the weather on the BBC; the English shake their heads, chuckle, smile. Also on TV: a documentary.* The Diamond Queen. *In the U.S., only four days before June 2, there is a Katie Couric special featuring interviews with William and Harry, among others (more than 7 million Yanks tune in). And then the displays: At Buckingham Palace, an exhibit of the queen's diamonds is readied, while the shopping channel QVC prepares a floral tribute to Elizabeth and Philip (right)—two 11-foot-high terra-cotta flower pots and 50 varieties of plants. England is a-bloom this spring like never before.*

THE PREVIOUS Diamond
queen, Victoria, simply never
could have conceived of such a
thing—not in her very wildest
imaginings. What this is, at left:
The "Face Britain" project, in
which illustrated self-portraits by
200,000 children are projected
onto Buckingham Palace to form
renderings of Queen Elizabeth.
It is hoped by the organizers at the
Prince's Foundation for Children
& the Arts that the effort will set a
record for the largest collaborative
artistic effort ever, but regardless:
It's quite a tribute, and sets just
the right tone—respectful, but also
colorful and fun—as London is
set to plunge into the big weekend.
All the exhibits are packing
them in—"The Queen: Sixty
Photographs for Sixty Years" out at
Windsor, "The Queen: Art and
Image" at the National Portrait
Gallery, "Queen Elizabeth II by
Cecil Beaton: A Diamond Jubilee
Celebration" at the Victoria and
Albert Museum (please revisit our
Beaton portfolio on page 52 for
a taste)—and the pubs and block
parties, too, are filling, for it is
now time to celebrate in earnest:
to raise a pint of bitter or a cup
of Twinings to the queen and all
that she has contributed, all
that she has weathered, all that
she represents. First up, for the
woman herself, who has loved
horses since she was a little girl: a
trip to the races.

NO ONE has ever seen the queen place a bet. She reads the Racing Post *every morning, and she has often been found at the track. She breeds her own Thoroughbreds and knows the names of the 30 horses that are kept in the stables at the Royal Mews. She herself loves to ride, as we have seen, and her longtime racing manager John Warren has told BBC Radio that she thinks about racing "every day of her life." On top of this, she is one of the richest people in the world, but she has never been caught floating so much as a fiver on a favorite or a hunch. Too bad, for on June 2 at Epsom Downs Racecourse outside of London she surely would have been tempted, at the propitious outset of the Jubilee weekend, to try her luck in the big-money Derby with a horse named Camelot. As fate would have it, Camelot came through, with jockey Joseph O'Brien up. (O'Brien, feeling positively kingly, also won the Diamond Jubilee Coronation Cup, aboard St. Nicholas Abbey, on this day, and is seen opposite, bottom, receiving just some of his spoils from Her Majesty.) Opposite, top: Three beefier blokes than young O'Brien call for the latest odds, perhaps, while keeping the queen (or her cardboard surrogate) company at Epsom. Above: The queen is in her twin elements (at the track, and in the royal box) and is happy as a clam.*

THE WORLD SALUTES. Opposite, top: British troops in Afghanistan toast their monarch on the eve of Jubilee. As the weekend dawns, it does so first Down Under, where in Perth, Australia, the Jubilee Kilt Run kicks off (bottom). This page, top: In India—like Australia, once of the British Empire and still of the Commonwealth—an elephant is decked out on June 3. Above: Edmund Fry, owner of Rose Tree Cottage, serves guests during a Jubilee tea party. On Portobello Road? No, in Pasadena, California—and remember, the Colonies once belonged to Britain, too.

ANDREW PARSONS/ZUMA

PETE DEWHIRST/DEMOTIX/CORBIS

CHRIS ISON/PA/AP

OLIVIA HARRIS/REUTERS

LOVELY QUEENS-IN-WAITING and *two guys who would be king, clockwise from opposite: Prince Charles joins a street party in London's Piccadilly district; two sisters from Ascot walk the Mall in London in their Union Jack dresses; a young girl takes part in the Union Jack Paper Hat Swindon Diamond Jubilee Celebrations; and a brother and sister get regal in Chichester.*

ANDY RAIN/EPA/CORBIS

THEODORE WOOD/CAMERA PRESS, LONDON

TIM HALES/AP

NATIONAL NEWS/ZUMA

ENGLAND FLOWS ON. In the grandest and most emblematic of Jubilee events, one that confirmed British grit when the rain came down and 1.2 million nevertheless turned out, a reported thousand boats took to the Thames in emulation of the Canaletto painting, which showed London during the peak of the empire. Today, kayakers and pleasure craft accompany the royal barge downstream toward Tower Bridge, but the grandeur quotient is approximate.

"Long to reign over us"
Queen Elizabeth II
60 years on the throne
. . . and counting!